T0165489

IN SEARCH OF LIGHT

(A COLLECTION OF POEMS)

Bengali: ALOK BORTIKAR SHONDHANEY

Author & Translator:

M. Hasan Imam

Order this book online at www.trafford.com
or email orders@trafford.com

Most Trafford titles are also available at major online book retailers.

© Copyright 2011 M. Hasan Imam.
All rights reserved. No part of this publication may be reproduced, stored in a retrieval
system, or transmitted, in any form or by any means, electronic, mechanical, photocopying,
recording, or otherwise, without the written prior permission of the author.

Printed in the United States of America.

ISBN: 978-1-4269-6152-6 (sc)
ISBN: 978-1-4269-6153-3 (e)

Trafford rev. 08/04/2011

 www.trafford.com

North America & international
toll-free: 1 888 232 4444 (USA & Canada)
phone: 250 383 6864 ♦ fax: 812 355 4082

Table of Contents

"In the little heart, the unending thirst
Not quenched, will not quench, hope will not be fulfilled."

*[This was my mom's memory touch
That was framed in glass in village home
Hanged on the beam of sitting room
In my very childhood.]*

Dedicated To:

The best of my life I could ever ask for, the greatest perseverance of my life, the name that is ominously engraved in the warmth of my memory, he is my dear father, Sujawat Ali Munshi (known as Munshi Shaheb), my dear mother, and to my dear sister's memory.

I am thankful to Jahangir who kindly took the time and helped me in Dhaka in formatting In Search Of Light for publication.

Reference: In Search of Light

A few words:

It is my belief that from the very start of my career as a writer, especially in the rhythm and body of poems, in vocabulary, in expressions, the human life, the daily social life, humanity and human rights issues come straight up over everything and want to stay alert to join in the time stream of eternity, to keep an eye on the life stream of all time, be it the neglected, oppressed, poor human or the cruel power of the oppressors.

Today, I am truly pleased in this thought that the long cherished devotion of mine is finally shaping up in reality through the publication of this selected cluster of poems, the name of which is *In Search of Light* (Bengali: Alok Bortikar Shondhaney). While I was living here abroad for many, many years, most of these poems have been written within that time period. With a great hope I have come so far to present my works to you. The works that have found place in this publication cover a period of over thirty years.

At this time junction, I have presented to you a part of my literary works of all those years. To that end, I am conceivably affirmed, delighted, excited and in humble silence, hopeful. I hope through the creations of these time periods, I shall have the opportunity to come close to you for the works that I have endeared for so long. The past ages and the works have spoken and now it is up to you to judge, to slice and to build, if it is to be so. Let the bell ring if it is to save human causes and thereby humanity.

I would also hope that in the tide of this publication, let it tremble, shiver, crumble and finally break down to ruins the workshop of those of the oppressors because of whose terrible thoughts, plans and diplomatic cruel deeds the innocent oppressed, repressed and tortured human of my devotion day by day sink to the bottom of their unblossomed life. Let them, the oppressed, be awakened and rise up with vigor into the tide of life at this moment.

M. Hasan Imam
Author

Other Published Books of this Author in Bengali

Total of Twenty-Two Publications of which all but Three are Poetry Books

1. In Search Of Light
Bengali: Alok Bartikar Shondhaney

2. In Devotion
Bengali: Onuragay

3. In Long Days Path
Bengali: Onak Diner Pothay

4. Going Singing
Bengali: Gaiey Jaie

5. Different Style
Bengali: Onno Rokom

**6. Named It A Mixed Taste
(Mixed
Collections)**
Bengali: Nam Rakhechi Misron Shud

7. Will Listen One Day
Bengali: Eik Din Hobay Shona

8. Just The Other Day
Bengali: Aieto Shadin

9. Framed Pain
Benjali: Badano Jontrona

10. Flow
Bengali: Probaho

11. In The Path Of Poem
Bengali: Kobitar Pothay

12. Standing In Front The Dream City,

New York **(Novel)**
Bengali: Somukhe Dondaoman
Shopner Rup Nogori, New York

13. America After Eleventh September
(Novel)
Bengali: America Agaru September Por

14. Suddenly In Different Mind
Bengali: Hodot Onno Monay

15. Deprived Solicitation
Bengali: Bonchito Ubdar

16. Doesn't Heed Stop Singing
Bengali: Guaite Manena Baron

17. Still Continued Asking
Bengali: Akhono Cholsey Juson

18. Anchored On The Shoulder of Man
Bengali: Munober Shioray Nungor

19. Entrapped Ardent Entreaty
Bengali: Ubodda Ukoti

20. Tie Free
Bengali: Badon Hara

21. Brightened In Silent
Bengali: Nirobe Utvasito

22. Wake Up In Wave After Wave
Bengali: Torongay Torongay Jagao

M. Hasan Imam: Author

M. Hasan Imam is the son of Hajigonj, Chandpur (Comilla), Banglasesh. He's an established Pharmacist in New York, a poet by nature, a novelist and a periodical writer. He currently has in his credit twenty-two publications of poetries and novels. This is not the only identity he has. Since his youth he's been a successful organizer both in his motherland as well as in New York.

He's been living in New York for three decades. Here, along with a devotion to literature, he was engaged in writing periodicals in different Bengali newspapers on economic and political aspects of Bangladesh and its people. He started writing since school life and has collections since 1969. Around that time, his writings started to come up in some national newspapers in Dhaka.

he joined in the liberation war in 1971 as a freedom fighter against Pakistani invaders. He was at the time a Senior Officer in the Quality Control Department of Pfizer Laboratories International. He was praised in those times because of his devotion to the human cause, like recovering in a go-down of the looted items such as gold, utensils, cattle, houses, etc. after they were identified in the worst possible looted area during the war as the chairman of the Freedom Fighters Society, Hajigonj and returning them to the real owners with sentry guards after the downfall of the Pakistani army in December 16th, 1971. He did this for about four months before rejoining Pfizer. At the same he was protecting the business institutions in Hajigonj from looting by providing around the clock sentry guard to those locations.

As a first batch student he earned B.Pharm (Hons) and Masters Degree in Pharmacy from Dhaka University, Bangladesh and got into the Ph.D. program at The University of Connecticut, Storrs Campus. After completing two years of course work and before starting research, due to financial hardships, he went back to New York and completed his RPH in 1980.

- Before coming to the USA he performed his duties as Quality Control Manager of Pfizer Labs International from 1971-1973. Also performed as Chairman, Drama Committee of Pfizer Family and staged, for the first time, a Drama in Engineers Institute for 2 nights. It was very well received throughout various newspapers. Under his guidance as the Chairman of the Bengali Translation Committee all official documents were translated into Bengali and formatted for future use.
- In New York he worked as the Inventory Control Manager in Ketchum Laboratories and as Plant Manager in Emgee Pharmaceuticals, both located on Long Island, 1977-1981.
- Founding General Secretary and writer of the constitution of the Jajigonj Thana Student Society, 1963-1964.
- Founding General Secretary and writer of the constitution of the Dhaka University Pharmaceutical Society, 1966-1967. Dr. habibur Rahman, a teacher of the dept, was the President of the organization.
- Founding General Secretary and writer of the constitution of Pharmacy Graduates Association (PGA), Bangladesh and a life sustainer as General Secretary through difficult times for five years, the Presidents were Mr. Wahed Ahmed, a Managing Director of Fisons Pharmaceuticals, and Mr. Salimullah, Managing Director of Jasons Pharmaceuticals, among others.
- Actively engaged in establishing the constitution and the organization of Bangladesh Pharmaceuticals Society after independence, before which it was Pakistan Pharmaceuticals Society, 1972
- President and General Secretary of the Bangladesh Society, New York, 1979-1984. Involved in activities for

about twenty years serving the Bengali community and the author of the accepted and approved full-pledged constitution of the Bangladesh Society, as the chairman of the constitution committee, in 2001, which he started working on in 1979.

- Chairman, FOBANA Constitution Committee and the author of the full-pledged FOBANA constitution.
- Author of the constitution of Farrakka International Committee, New York.
- Founding General Secretary and President of Bangladesh forum of North America for eight years, and the author of its constitution, as chairman of the constitution committee, 1987 and up.
- He is the creator of the Evergreen famous name, the 'Embassy Building' located on Highland Avenue in Jamaica Queens, 1979. In those days this was the only building with the highest concentration of Bangladeshis at one location after the Bangladesh Embassy. That's how he started addressing the building and writing in society's magazines and eventually, it got the name in 1979.
- He was one of the main personalities to organize a demonstration in front of the United Nations under the banner of the Bangladesh League of America in 1973 for repatriation of Bangladeshi POWs and civilians who got held up in Pakistan after the Liberation War in 1971.
- He was the energy and main organizer to form the Committee for Democracy in Bangladesh outside the platform of Bangladesh Society, New York to organize a protest in front of the United Nations against the invitation of the then military ruler Ershad Hossain to speak in the upcoming general assembly of the United Nations in 1982.
- While a Ph.D. student at UConn, Storrs, he was the president of international students at International House, director of which was Dr. Knapp at that time.

THE MORNING BREEZE

Bengali: 'Vorer Shomiron'

Ah! What a peace it brings
Cool and contentful this freedom-breeze
Upon the dew drops of the morning
That culminates soft shiver of joy unto the world.

As if, tiredful hard laborious revolutions of ages
Have brought in the flank of ruined unpeaceful nights
The soft-lit flooded peace
Into its own overwhelmed blessings of morning breeze.
After years of inflicted sorrows it seems
With sequel of pious and pure devotion
This morning breeze has come into this world again.

September 12, 1970
Shiddeshssori, Dhaka,
Bangladesh

EMPTINESS GROWS BIGGER AND BIGGER

Bengali:
'Shunnota Burre Shudhu Burre'

(In memory of my father)

It seems only that day I took my seat
In the Baby-Taxi-,
The very known face for a long time, deeply rooted memory
Has given tears in the language of goodbye,
The instantly touched mind grew restless in silent motion,
In the open Baby-Taxi, the village-town wind
Gently flows------,
In the open door of my heart
I left him behind-
Emptiness grows bigger and bigger.

Here, I crossed over many paths
In the soothing cold stream of river
"Launches" are swimming -
Lots of people with lots of courages
Like though, in the corner of a tin-shed house
Clusters of Shalik birds live-
Going and going
Far far away-

Lots of crowd, Rickshaws and people
Horns of cars startles every one,

All of it like a fair, play of far distance
Be off-
Going and going
Emptiness grows bigger and bigger.

Ah, here it is, a big plane
Even bigger is the vacuum, flies over
The Aeroplane-,
Crossing over the seas, the vast lands
The human habitations--,
And of birds animals as well
Have gone far far away,
The dream lands of clouds in the sky
by evading them--
A retreat from the mind
Emptiness grows bigger and bigger.

Years come round and around
That look and silent expression
Peeps over my mind
My memory resounds,
The rhythm of past life
Came round and around and slept away,
The heat of summer does not feel that strong
Now-a-days--,
Next door to the bungalow flows
The Dakatia--,
The flood of full moon descends there like before
Only Vutiali in that old tune
Does not come floating,

That same fast stream of Dakatia flows
But no sound-

Who is going to listen to-day
I am but in the lonely room of a foreign land
Keeping awake.

M. Hasan Imam

October 13, 1980
Brooklyn, New York

[In memory of my dear Dad while coming to America at time of good-bye.]

Notes:
Launch--A passenger transport in water smaller than steamer
Baby-Taxi--Three wheeled small taxi for passengers
Richshaw--Three wheeled bike-transport for people
Shalik - a kind of small birds
Dakatia -- Name of a river
Vutiali -- Boat people's song

CAREFUL TO CROSS THIS SLIPPERY PATH

Bengali: 'Shubdhunay Perute Hobay Aitookoo Pichchill Poth'

High mountain, - the aches, griefs and sorrows of deprived and
have nots
Have accumulated here and became dense, - dazzles
At the reflection of schorching sun light-.
It takes the appearances of sharply slippery with revolting heat
And oppressed shouts as if wants to burst out.

When the burning heat of soul becomes unbearable
Pain and sorrows come down the body of mountain
continuously --
Gradually melts down the accumulated innerself-cry
In the shape of crying water--,
And rolls down to the main public through fare, still shiny and
bright-
The wealthy and aristocratic cars become startled
At the sight of this dazzling fluid, --bring down the speed
And become very awaken and cautious --
Lest they fall upside down in this slippery path of sorrow and
pain.

While going, they perhaps look back up for a moment
The dazzling white reflections of pain and sorrows

Make their eyes feel dizzy,
The humanity soul of civilization slowly turns foggy
Only then, turn their eyes quickly away--,
A shiver of fear peeps through their mind.
In the twinkling of their thought they encounter uncomfortable
frenzy
Must cross this little slippery path, --they murmur
Carefully very carefully.

March 13, 1981
Brooklyn, New York

LANGUAGE OF THE HUNGRY

Bengali: 'Khhuduthher Vusha'

The soft red morning glow
Kissed the bossom of the earth
And said, hello! I am rising
……… Sun-.

Said, I came to
Save you from the dark-depth,
With this thought I put my
……….Step-.

Your burned-out soul, oppressed
Human-heart gives me pain,
The Ruler-King, listen to the sorrows of the hungry, I
………..Pleade-.

But the King is deeply absorbed ruling
Busy allover, for whom
Nobody knows, only followers and ministers are
………..Happy-.

May 31, 1993
Port Washington
New York

BIRTHDAY CELEBRATON

Bengali: 'Jonmodiner Utshov'

Since the dawn of spring or even before that
Countless blooming times
Have passed by--
The accosting birthday cake didn't hold
The light of candles.

The time has come climbing down the seasons steps
And has gone with the pulling of tide,
The resurrection of birthday did never happen in close vicinity.

The workful life walking over the body of life.
Has made me forget the count of birthdays,
I have survived and am surviving
From the morning east-horizon I only pulled the grinder
To the setting horizon of the West untiringly.

Today, suddenly you all, by catching me in birthday celebration melee
Has brought shame upon my whole person,
I, in the company of millions of birthday less homes
Was the light of lightless,
In whose homes the usurer walks, or-
Who with their children are quietly helpless and hopeless
Whose only hope is to pull their lives relentlessly.

September 14, 1996
Port Washington, New York

THE INDEBTEDNESS
TO AKUSHE

Bengali: 'Akusher Pauna'

At the door is Fulgoon, the blood of my brother
The success and accumulated pain of 21st February.
Again, will come eye catching banquoet of flowers
Cleverly strung in multitude design, bunch after bunch
Stay lying in rows at the foot and soul of martyr-tower
Eye-catching arrangements bearing identity of those-selves.

Some are leaders, some parties of political and students alike,
Some are cultural groups, colleges and universities, all banded
Aristocratic flowers golup, mollika, muloti, rogoni Gondha, Bakuls
Airing fragrances and away hearts but the Minar gets worried
It murmers, some politicians among these in disguise of lover
Put garland upon me but in the back bring the doom of country.

This honour of those burns me in licking fire,
The people's property and right are being robbed by these in the
name of Akushe,
My brother's food are seized by them from their mouth,
These are deceitful, murderer and group's of smugglers
In the face they are country-lover politicians, smilingly lay down
the trap of trust.

You, who are blood bathied and now at my foot and soul
Know them and don't be carried away at the bounty of their flower
banquets,
I didn't want these banquets crushed with people's hopes and lives,
To have beared me in memory, the honour of these flowers will be
worth then-
When the meaning and demands of martyr's bloods will be realized
and fulfilled.

February 13, 1993
Port Washington
New York

Notes:
Minar - Martyr Tower
Akushe - 21st Feb. Bengali Language martyrs Day

FLOATING

Bengali: 'Vhushomun'

In the playground upon green grass
I lay seated --
The pen is about to walk on white paper.

Unnoticed, - on my paper
Comes repeatedly flying shadow
The affection of the sky of distantly flying hawk.

I feel mind only floats
By creating waves
In ether after ether--.

August 2, 1997
Long Island, New York

PASSING THIS WAY

Bengali: 'A Pothey Jetee'

So many times, I thought, While passing this way
That I'll sit by this bank
Some morning when crows are cawing
And when the water recedes with fallen tides.

So varieties of stones and remnants of their bodies,
On some, algaes have drawn it's color impressions
Some have sprinkles of sands, some have spots
Some have droplets of water sticking to their bodies.

I'll collect all these kinds while limping over, walking slowly
Lest my feets get tainted with algae-muds and sands,
Lots of variety shells scattered around besides stones
Broken are their faces and bodies and their beauty faded.

So many days, I thought
Stepping on these sands, stones, shells and water sprinkles scattered
I'll walk down far away where
Down tide ends and the continuity of water proceeds to endless streams.

Lots of stalks, seguls come and sit in this broad sphere,
In the morning glare of sun light
They gently caress their wings with their beaks
Some walk dancingly polite catching the eyes to admire.

So many times, I thought, having seated at this bank
I'll swallow the enchanting feelings of water touching floated
Innumerable boats and on their bodies
The embracing beauty of morning sun with the intimate reflections
of water.

So many days, I thought, the beauty of this path
Has to be entrenched under my feet in cool touch
Into my body and then to be engraved into my heart
While walking on the sands stones and their remnants through
collection of pleasure

I only keep passing this way
Over and over again in this path
Have no leisure only thoughts come back again and again
The more I think, the hope only remains in sea-sand of thoughts.

November 4, 1997
Port Washington, N.Y.

NEWLYRISEN CHARACTERTREE

Bengali: 'Nobudoe Choritrobrikhho'

I planted this tree with care
Many years passed now, -- in the year 1757
Named it 'Charactertree', will be
Like Bot-gus (Banyan tree), the tree-root will spread for
Collection of juice in the fertile subterranean
Pocket ---.

The branches will spread branch-root
Floating in the air it will fill
The heart, with the collection of juice
The harvest will be bountiful. Like
The leaves, they will bear large fruits
Tasty ---.

From aside Botbrikhho, in this fashion
It is only different, all other's
have similarity. Inside the fruits
Caressed like cells of jackfruits,
The appearance of each cell is
Different---.

In the light of experience, they are
Connected, separately
In the same fruit like the same
Stalk-. Over two hundred of
Years passed upon Choritrobrikhho but still
Firm---.

Like the Cactus of Arizona
Hundreds of years of desert storm
Has passed
Over it, Cactus has
Nourished this experience at it's root,
Body---.

In the courtyard of this world, choritrobrikhho
Grew through difficult time,
Eighteen hundred and fifty seven passed,
Upon the decadence of colonialism, descended
Storms and clouds, even 1947 on the strike of 1952
Fledaway---.

The Fruits of seventy one came brightened
In the branch of Choritrobrikhho, the cells are
Radient, the roots rich in accumulated juice
With profound wisdom, the whole body full of promises
Brimming in green leaves
To create ----.

Over two hundred years
Storms passed over this tree-body,
Roots have given hopes,
Holding heart tight, - Shades
Will give rest and peace, --with this
Expectation ---.

M. Hasan Imam

The curse has come upon Choritrobrikhho again
Like ages and ages before
Leaves are falling off due to malnutrition
For the common people, there is no shades,
No shelter while on the road,
On the way to bazaar--, for a moment's
Rest ---.

The Borgies are gone, the deudal statetism is absent,
Some vulture-like creatures
Still sit on the branches, imperialism is
Beyond border, there are some indigenous elements
the deceptive artifice persecution of politicians,
Untimely storm of Boishakh, --- Choitro, in the tree
Inerned ---.

With the rotation of time, Choritrobrikhho shedded
The slough to uproot the nail-markings of
Thunder-bolt, A new body came
Again with new vigor.
Time has come, this time around also will shed
Slough ---.

My compound now, is, suffocated,
The absence of peaceful embodiment and it's viewless vigor
In the Choritrobrikhho bring mockery to it's
Two hundred years of experience, ---gives me pain--,
The root's yet didn't give up hope
Still ---.

And it's spreading deeper in the try for more juices
To derive, in disguise more new
Capillaries are taking shapes to collect
Juices, the demand of life is moving forward
In silence, in depth, in touch with
Cool soil in Chritrobrikhho under the name
New-Bangladesh-.

February 28, 1996
Port Washington, New York

Notes:
Choritrobrikhho.. Chractertree
Choitro... The last month of Bengali year (tuff summer days)
Boishakh...Bengali first month borgious..maharstha cavalries..the notorious
invaders.

NAKED WALL

Bangali: 'Bibosro Deuli'

It is written in this wall--,
You are lying down
On the other sided of this wall
beneath the ground --.

Yellow leaves dry out in afflicted sorrows,
Dropping on your chest,
Tired air goes hish hish
In the ear of memory--.

Only me standing here, --naked,
The strike of corrupted power of freedom turned it so.
Thoughts come to cross over,
The wall is too high and just can't jump over.

October 6, 1997
Long Island, New York

YOUR ORDER

Bengali: 'Tomar Uddesh'

One day in that vaccum in the blue sky
By drawing the surroundings of thrilled supernatural bindings
The way the shape-engulped personality body of 'MUFASA'
Came floating into the clouds--,

If you youeself likewise, suddenly with bodied-soul
Would have appeared covering the sky with finger pointing,
The drifting trend towards the doom of this mankind worldwide
May have been saved.

Perhaps the Sharp directives of your finger,
The order reflections would have brought wisdom
At the root of this society, in the brain kingdom of rulers.

If that wouldn't have been enough in this ignorant villa
I was always ready--,
From that time in the past
Waiting for your order.

I would have engraved at the root of all encampments of injustices
Your order that is dissolutionsless over eternal peaks.

March 20, 1997
Long Island, New York

Notes MUFASA - Actor hero of
'Lion King' movie

TEST

Bengali: 'Porikkha'

Ok, Go ahead
Finish thyself,
What it is to burn yourself like husks
To draw the end of oppressed heart,
Instead, what a thrill it is to shut the life suddenly!

I told you---
These are all rats, termites and cowdung worms
The healthily grown flies and mosquitoes in dirts nourishments
Will sit in your body and flash
And will suck your juice out in comfort, tear you off and eat
Like homeless hungry vultures
The hope of your life.

I told you---
These are low cadre tonsured dogs, --suddenly
Coming out of bush
They are like frenzied running wild foxes,
Like heat strickened swirling
Lunatic stray -dogs of the street--
Your hopeless vigour, weak from all-lost body and mind of yours
They will bite out even the last support of your life.

I warned you--
Don't go ahead with very little defense at your hand,
The easily gotten depth of flash

And accumulated severe foul smelled magnetic attraction
Has hooked them up into addiction
Like nothing could resist them.

With one sudden paw they will drag you down
To the bottom of that life-killer fouled-smelled heap
You may never sense the place of your existence.

I told you--
These society-destroyer worm people
Are crazy for the blood
of the poor, the middle class, school going class, the general
people.
Irrespective of nation, age, society and religion
In the safe heaven of security of the rullers
Many of these have tunnel like connections,
As though, the line of ants with diamonds in their mouths
Enter into the hidden hole underground.

Nope! All these terrible consequences
The prayer and warning of engulfed burned soul
The blazing licking tongue of fire of the darkness
And the bitter pain of their poisonous bites
Nothing could stop you!

I urged you don't go, beware--
In this battle you will loose your person and your life,
You smiled silently and politely, leaning down--
With heavenly brightness in your eyes and face
Not caring the fear at all!

I shivered with pride and dignity
Lava-tears burst out of my eyes
With eternal respect towards your turbulent look
With directional blessings of guiding stars.

In fact it was not meant to stop you
It was only a test for you from me.

August 1, 1997
Port Washington, New York

IN A DIFFERENT LOCALITY

Bengali: 'Ovinno Parrai'

When my poem saw the bullet-wound afflicted body
Lying down motionless at the cooking house frontyard
Of Gedu Mia, the next door neighbour---,
It didn't break down into pieces.
Without being perturbed by the scenarios, it, on the outer house
Of Munshi Bari, announced the event.
In two sides, are crops fields, on their back was built
High road through which it reached to Gopal-Para,
After passing the clusters of banana trees.
It came across and passed cowdung scattered paths of milky cow-
houses
And announced the scenarios to the Puja warshipers in their
Mondirs.

Coming back in the high road again,
In the front is the main gate of Molla Bari,
The people who just finished praying in the mosque,
And, in the name of Allah started on the road or towards the inner
house,
It let them know--
The news of the dead body--,

Coming out of the main gate,
It crossed over three corners of the high-road
And arrived at the front of Patwari-Bari where lines of Shegoon
trees stand up-right,

Which, in turn, touches the big pond next to it,
It's where it announced the bullet story to the gathered people.
A hue and cry rose up in locality after locality--
But the poem didn't get scared.

Even on the threat of those-,
A gathering was taking place of all, young and old alike.
In a grave but high and deep tone
It ignited the inner torch
From this very stage of this village
Which was built in moments--,
You have to stand up to oppose injustices
And you have got to know who is your real friend of heart,
Who comes quietly indisguise of a close one
Persuing the act of a good-man in keenly alliance,
You will erect your own
Truthful representative who will establish your rights.

Delivering this message the poem
Head-started for another locality
Like the speedy ship of a different planet in the sky.

November 3, 1997
New York

Notes:
Munshi Bari, Molla Bari...Name of village house, Mosque...
Prayer house for Moslems (Islam), Gedu Mia.. Name Gopal
Para. Name of a locality, Puja warshippers.. Hindu prayers
Hindu Mondir. Temple for Hindus It.. Poem,

YOUR GREATNESS

Bengali: 'Tomur Mohotto'

I know mankind is doing wrongs
In seas, in lands all the time,
behind the people's eyes most often--
But to deceive, to go behind you
Who have no power--,
Where they will hide?
They are bloated, stckingly attached
Mixed into the cells of your body and mind.

All the improper and wrong doings
Are stationed, that's why, within the boundary of your vision,
you see them, --but
Tolerate them into your heart
In the little corner of your endless tolerance vassel,
You keep awake with an invitation of forgiveness,
With one drop from your vast domain of forgiveness
You sprinkle the mankind,
Their burning sin-souls get cleaned up
Upon repenting through your cool pardon touch.

That this rule of play, as it is
It seems --
Your hide and play act, it looks.
That you are the greatest
The final endless vast vassel of forgiveness, the holiest places of all

That's what you're proving and make it prove
In the mind of mankind--.

You indulge in the tendency of their wrong doings
And then, forgive the mankind for the same
Attaching the technique of how to ask for forgiveness.
Your greatness you yourself
Are proving again and again,
The treasure of endless eternal forgiveness
Holding in your hand.

December 24, 1997
Port Washington, New York

BLESSED THIS LIFE

Bengali: 'Dhonno a-Jibon'

Touch me, cool me down
The Morning breeze --
Open up my inner heart
The enchanted eyes --

My entire body, heart and mind
Let reverberate --
The burden of all my sins until death
Be removed and shook off--

For ages this heart is thirsty, in closeness
Longed for you--
All over the heart the diver searches days and nights
In all exhaustion assembly --

Tell me the greatest one (you)
The savor of all world ---
Your blessings I place over my head
This life is always thankful --

December 24, 1997
Port Washington, New York

NEGLECTED DEATH

Bengali: 'Obohelito Mritto'

This is the way you embrace death, __you
In the headline of new papers
Become picture of news --
May be not even that--.

Being chained up in the repeatedly licking thurst of blazing death,
In every day news
In the curious eyes of the early morning
You become the news of talk.

That's all --,

Within the difference of couple of days
You get lost
From the page of news, --gradually
From the minds of compassionates,
And the minds of the rest in advance
Keep awaiting to forget.
With you goes the history of your neglected life
In the welcome house of God.

After that --,

In Search Of Light

The cold eclipse of long waited death
Guards your children, wife and your parents
The dependent family members,
With a hand-wave of sympathy,
And embraces, then, into the soundless nights
Of unknown swing of difficult breathing --.

As you swing, at one time
These of you become tired in your eyes
And get leaned at the back of the swing.
Then you go faded gradually and get lost in silence
From the familiar faces of the society, the roads, the path
From the familiar house, surroundings--,

The active society, the rulers, ruling courts even by mistake
Did not look back!

(Thoughts on the death in the blaze of garments factory in Dhaka,
Bangladesh)

August 9, 1997
Long Island, New York

CONFLICT AT HUMAN SHORE

Bengali: 'Munob Kulay Shonghut'

I'm on the road, going. A thought sheltered
On my shoulder while walking. I am
Now face to face with the junction of multidirectional roads,
Thinking of the young boys and girls of Dulmain School
Of Scotland village. The strike of automatic weapon

Gunned down sixteen young lives
In the cold casket of death, like the ducks in the sky
Shot down by the hunter and
Fell on the ground lifeless. Their wide open eyes
Only throwing questions non-stop
At the killer human and
At the conscience of civilized world.

At this junctions of all roads, the machine monsters
Are cris-crossing fast without paying heed to the pedestrians.
Only suddenblust of dusts
Like sudden gusts of air against my body are
Pounding around my wrapped up dresses--

And are fleeing away then; Again-
I get lost in my thoughts and reach the home of
That unfortunate woman whose teenager girl
Was kidnapped and then killed after rapping
Like animals leaving sign of torture

All around the body. These killers are human too,
Indisguise of human they walk around in the society
Concealing their barbarious animal-ferociousness.
The law of civilized society set these human-monsters
Free on pay-roll, save them under the guise of insanity,
By engaging state lawyers for them.
The care for killers under the ultraviolet lens of laws
Are far more highly appreciated with sympathy and fellow-
Feelings, The one killed and
The tremendous loss of their families, the mourning of
Loss for loosing the Victim, all those are valueless,
The law show them pity! Kidnapping and killings
And their results have taken shelters in the book of no-acconts.

At the junctions-face of all roads, the air is now
Indisciplined, haphazard; someone in mean while
Said, Hi- and then vanished,
Turning in that side I found myself
Alone in the midst of many. --In Long Island,

In this multi-facial corner of human society the sudden air
Whispered into my ear the incident of a mother
Who has cut off the memory of childrearing time
As if with a sharp knife the way they cut
The green young healthy leaves of esculent plant, the same way
Two little sons were belted on into the seat of car by their mother,

And then, the running car was let go into the dish-pond.
The two childs were kidnapped, this message was
Publicized by mother to the neighbours and the police station.
Upon the shameful face of mother the faces of two dead boys
Come afloat from the bottom of dish-pond at day-end cruelty!

Suddenly I noticed, held in my hand is
A pen and a pad, In this multifacial junction of roads,
Standing in surprise in the Kingdom of thoughts,
I couldn't find which messenger of civilization
Has planted into my hand-

This sword of pen on the paper of mango-grove-garden.

March 24, 1996
Port Washington, New York

GIVE ME BACK AGAIN

Bengali: 'Ubur Firea Dao'

This lane is very familiar to me,
It didn't seem in my heart that I've mistaken to recognize it.
I walked down this lane innumerable times in my childhood
When, in the face of the youth, a very thin line of
Mustache begins to grow like needles in fine décor,
This known path with sharp look
Have witnessed that vibrant growth in me.
The air was pellucid then, easy comfortable life in two sides.

I paid a visit to that lane to-day mistakenly loosing directions,
In depth desire of mind what is that vibration of feeling!
I felt myself to be getting reduced
Like a horror toy transformer-.
The translucent air has taken goodbye from this lane.
As well, the easy going life of my hopeful beloved human.
As if, due to the romping of demon of distant evil planet
The dear familiar lane has transformed into a barbage place.

In the face of child, youth, young & old, a mystic cry is visible,
In their look an impression of fear, as though, has gotten painted
Like that from a printing press. In place of clean translucent life
A ledger museum of poverty has taken place.
In a definitive dark corner of the lane
In the thin shade of lamp post light
The welcome smiles of young girls give a signal of different path,

In the past healthy curvature of the body, now the number of bones
are vividly clearer.

A suspicion took hold of my mind about the identity of this lane
The lost 'Moina' bird of mine
Suddenly came around from no-where,
Gave a round over my head
And started speaking, I extended my hand in the air,
It landed in there, -the body has become very sickly and thin all-
around,
And somewhat discoloured too, Moina assured me
'You didn't make mistake, my friend, this known lane is yours,
Only the selfish conflict of blind humans
Indisguise of rulers and opposition's claims
Have snatched away the honourful translucent life of this lane'.

Having reciting so, my Moina bird
Said, 'Good by-, if you can do it again
Give me back my old lane I'll come back to earth'.

April 29, 1996
Port Washington, New York

TESTED BY HEART

Bengali: 'Porikkhito Ridoer'

You have traveled this way with serious austere devotion of mind
Like the unending fall from a fountain
You have embraced the stream of rain,
Disregarding the schorching heat of the sum
In a burned out body
You have accepted the pain of burned skin
With a smiling face--,

At one time, in a field full of crops that it was
The drought has befallen the fields,
It has spread cutting breaking them into pieces, in the sky
The way it gets cut on flashes of lighning
Upon your chest cutting, curving and engraving,
Still you are fearless amidst the storm
Moving forward--.

Your cottage, all around
Is under water up to the neck,
Like small pieces of islands
Amidst endless inundated areas
You are at the top of a little cottage
Keeping your head high, and
Amusing the play of eternal water--,

Who can give you pledge of security and safety
You and you only are it's birth giver,
A very little caress affection, lifeless though, of this civilization
May manage the audacity to touch you!

You are noble with pride
Has given wisdom to mankind
Tested by heart.

June 15, 1996
Port Washington, New York

IN THE WAVE RISES LIFE-POEMS

Bengali: 'Dheoa Jugay Jibon Kobita'

To you-
Poems make feel good, you said--
Surrounded by the cool shades of forests
The attractions of mind with their divine entities
Take you into the depth, thereafter--

Keeping you sitted into the thought-stool,
Like, in the palms of both sides of both hands
The skilled decorative work of Mindi
With it's illuminating wonder of painting
Take you into
The wave of beauties of fancied bride-room.

Like, getting a new life, you--
Are thrilled in arbor boscage,
In the ups and downs rhythm of word-combinations of poems
And in it's friendly oscillating wave you
Float around as poem
Universe to universe
In the company of stars and planets.

July 26, 1997
Long Island, New York

Notes:

Mindi - Hand decorating paste of green leaves used in Indian-subcontinent by girls

LION - STRIKE

Bengali: 'Shingho Ughut'

An impossible plan I have adopted in my mind.
Sitting at the shore of the ocean, - where
Incessant water of broken waves after climbing it's peaks
Have dispersed it's self conviction of gravity,
The lust of all bounty, where-
By touching the shells transforms into one
Unbelievable beautiful city, -- In that
shore of sands at the courtyard of widespread diversity,
From the heart of endless ocean came flying
A white calm goose
Spreading it's wide wings in the sky.

It came down and sat on my shoulder,
Addressing in a polite guesture
Into my ear, - offered me
It's good blessings--,
Told me while saying good-bye,
'Don't forget, the dictionary of injustices are growing high
Towards all human,
Like the notorious effects of Farakka
The human soul is falling sprawling on the ground here & there,
In many guises inland and in far land, -- it said
'Don't forget the proportion of injustices,
Put in order the plan of lion-strike.

August 1, 1996
Port Washington, New York

THIS LIFE THIS PAIN

Bengali: 'Aei Jobon Aei Betha'

When the good-by took it's effect
It is more than two decades now,
In a clean pellucid body of mine came down then
Feelings of pain alleviated pure consolation
In depth of my mind the trensands of fright has taken exit.

I am relieved and alive
This was the conclusion of my clean-cut thought.

Back it came to-day
The pain of society with the pain of my vein
Has taken alliance.
I want to have pain alleviated conclusion
I would like to see that the spark of my pain
With the pain that is engraved in the back and lap of society
Has taken leave forever.

My mind wants to get relief and live
By removing and dispelling the starvation of crores of people all over
I want to see
In a highly pleased celestial ray of splendour
Seated I am.

And they --
Are in full bloom in the cheerful triump-song of life.
Are no more worried and preoccupied in the thoughts of foods,
Clothes & shelters.
Are not pounded, smashed and bruised in
befallen thoughts
They are also alive and living well.

December 28, 1996
Long Island, New York

HYENAS OF BOSNIA, - STOP

Bengali: 'Bosniar Hyena Thumo'

Bosnia, your beautiful name Yugoslavia is parallel to ghost to-day.
These trees, river, swamp, the green attractions of top of mountain
They also loose lives under the aggression of ruining-forests
Human are responsible for these mishaps like Surbs, Life
Wakes up again in the congregation of greenness; In the lava of
volcanoes
Blood-red flames roll down. The crests of green forests mixed with ashes
Rise up from the heart of Ruins,
Again life comes up.

Bosnia, in your chest, to-day---
Vulture gathered partying, they are killers, flesh eaters.
In the name of human, they are overpowered by ghosts
In the veins of their heads. That's why your clean body
Is bloodied to-day, no affection, justices are only the plunge of
wings of Vultures,
This river, these trees, mountains are shameful in your chest to-day,
Do the trees have religion? No, -only has name.
Do the mountains, rivers have religion? No, --not really.
They have songs of life and it's name is heart.

Bosnia, your vessel is empty to-day, indigent, muddied,
In the history of humanity you are paws of hyenas to-day, dirtied,
Your bloodied killer-hands, Serb, where would you hide?

These trees, these rivers & these mountains, will they wash your
sins every time!
This is religion not names, only a way to live life.
You were like these trees, rivers before,
Suddenly you pleasure from killing
In your eyes, is explosion of blood thirst; You are less than human,
Wake up again like these rivers, trees.

May 23, 1993
Port Washington, New York

ARE THEY HUMAN!

Bengali: 'Era Ki Munoosh'

Are they human! Do their life
Has any value at all to Western World!
They are not human, rather, up in the middle of two legs
A heart was placed that walks!
They are in Bosnia, in Palestine country, in Africa
They are Lebanese, in the guise of minority in India,
They are a kind of 'life' (creature), the hunger of Somalia,
They are not Iraqis under oppression of queer.

The proud civilization of America and Europe and
In it's glass lens, they are human like
Transparent creatures; in the ridicule tapping of intension & gesture
They could be played around for nothing on self whimsicality.
Who says they are dying because of pain of oppression,
They are like a tool to test-run amusing tests
The same way you can do with mosquitoes
By pressing them between finger-tips & breaking apart their whole
intestine

They are not human that they will feel pain!
Never, - in the Europe-American civilization
Even the dogs and cats are more human,
Live in much adore and affection,
To their hungry tongue and greedy look
Who can give trouble, they sleep in the bed

Lick the cheeks of their masters
And give loving kisses in the naked lips of civilization.

These are - their human; in care, in pleasure
They are full to brim, breathe in the smell of meat
Their separate fresh foods are attractive to the eyes
The bonie-bodied people of so-called uncivilized nations
Could have lived on, such is the taste of look,
The civilized dog sleeps in the fat of peace.

Bosnia, Palestine, Lebanese and so more
Are they human? Let that be known.
Like toy-foam of America and Europe, - in their blow
They whirl around in twisted bangle,
They are like insignificant beings, the civilized cats & dogs
Are much more human compared to them.
And wealthy oil miner of Middle East
Licks the tail of the civilized.

August 6, 1993
Port Washington, New York

VESSEL OF FOOD

Bengali: 'Khaberer Udhur'

Under the compressed Pressure of hunger
the blood in the vein, as if, forms blue lotuses,
The tube is being inserted through the mouth into the stomach
The lips with little signal arouse expectation for food.

All around is pin-drop silence, - no revolt
Only pity in the unseen slum-huts of hair-follicles
Brought down cold touch-
In this dug-in soundless motionless room.
The world is deep drowned in darkness
The electric bulb, only, is the vessel of food.

June 21, 1996
Port Washington, New York

PALE DARKNESS

Bengali: 'Biborno Udhur'

They look like human in shape and build
How Wonder! In reality --
They are human in their entirety,
Like a fresh pure blossom in the stalk,
Ah! how soft and heavenly like a full moon
Transcending sinless and pious feelings.

Freshlly blossomed but rejected
In the dustbin, in the toilet, in Motel buskets
sometimes covered with plastics here and there and left alone.

Life is their in the body or, may be not
Crying or, may not be --
Only awake is the body or the two eyes
Lying down in His supernatural arms,
They bring pity to mankind
Upon these beneath profoundly degraded hateful events.

The newly born does not know whose child or whose womb bore it
Only throws questions at the divine shelter
Did you notice how far depth are the sins!

There is no delivery room but there is delivery
Sign of which is no where --
There is no sign of compassion nor affection

The human conscience in it's delirious form
Is being thrown in the island of drain-dirts.

In the domain of what an unthinkable cruelty, or --
Upon inspired by disorganised deranged morbid lust of aspirations
In the wicked sexual perverted condition of mind
This act of mischeap keep going round.

In another puzzle, -- you brought speculations
And abandoned an unfortunate human
In utter drive of poverty, may be you cried as well,
Yet forgiveness is not there in this apportionment
He who gave means look for that gift!

In this sphere of world in fertile or non-fertile sprout
The birth cord of the newly born
Still adhere to the path of vision
Touches the deluded aliveness in the diffused darkness.
(Thought conceived from the new borns being
deserted/thrown away in places of USA and other areas)

August 15, 1997
Long Island, New York

PERSEVERANCE

Bengali: 'Shudhona'

My, this perseverance walks along
Under lemon tree, Shimul, Polash, the Mudhobi Lota
Climbing down their deserted hearts through
The yellow garden of luxury of the evening. In the bank of green--
The rose, Molika, Muloti, Jasmine flowers
In their helpless timid softness,
On the roof tin-sheds where leaves are engaged in friendships,
Where full-moon light is drived away with the engulfing moonless
darkness.

In the raw smells of fresh leaves of jute plant fields
In the wave of green paddy fields with golden crops peeping
through
The persons who walk down the midst of these in agony with
burden of poverty
My perseverance walks along with their breaths.

In the villages, markets, in the stoves of countless human
The heartfelt pain of insufficient foods in the covered pots
From the cooking of which come out the visible vapours
That, in disguise, gives the consolation of real hope of plenty of foods
In the hungry curious looks of their children,
The past healthy body that walks now towards village markets
Showing the number of ribs in their bodies, a sign of fruits of post-
independence rules,

M. Hasan Imam

Come back from the market with half empty buskets in their hands,
My perseverance round and around
Returns at the site of their existence.

In the center of Indra of my perseverance, the lightning sound of
longing echoes--
If even, a green leaf can be saved
From being becoming yellow--,
If even a yellow leaf
could be kept alive from being dead drooping,
If even, a pillar could be protected
From being attacked by the deadly termites--,

If this very moon light of this very nation
could be carried to each home, even a drop of it--,
If with the full touch of this rain
A very little bit of pain of innumerable human
Could be alleviated--,

Then, at least, one dropfull of weight of this sea of pain and
sorrows
Will become lesser from loadfull burden of mankind.

October 3, 1997
Long Island, New York

Notes:
Shimul, olash, Mudhobi Lota, Mollika, Multo = Different kind
of enchanting smelly flowers.
Jute plant = At one time golden fibre plants of the world, now
mostly replaced by artificially developed rayons, fibres..etc.

NOT HIGHWAY ONLY

Bengali: 'Shudhu Highway Noy'

Do you think, by the side of highway
All the known have dwellings
Within a very short touch! -- that
Upon wish, leaving all the world-things behind
You can hide within glance
In the decorative black top corridors of the closed ones.

The periphery of the world would have, then, been shortened
The distribution of endless boundary
Would have lost sanctifying graces; the spreading of green
branches
In the unknown Mohalla of dense curiosity of locality
Would not have been vibratlly-bloomed,
The utter drowning of the curious mental presentation
Would have covered the earth at the boundary-side of the highway.

Life is not only surrounding the highway
It's definitive circumferences need to be passed,
To a little distant, at further distant in a quiet locality
Where green trees and birds nests
Have descended slowly touching the ground,
An unifinished human habitants have joined hearts,
There, also, hearts smile, talks
The blessings of God sprinkles amid land after lands,

In there too, life goes on in the knotted swings of affection
May be, there isn't much wealth but there is wilderness,
May be, there is everything but some are irrelevant
Not like the glamour of highway,
Still, krishnokoli talks, joba smiles
Thought peeps that the world is so beautiful, so near!

May 22, 1996
Port Washington, New York

Notes:
Krishnokoli/Joba: A kind of fragrant flowers.
Moholla: A segment of living area.

THE GREATEST MOTHER OF HEARSAY

Beangali: 'Kingbodontir Shera Ma'

The 'Nobel' of the Academy is lean and small
Upon the sky high person of yours--,
Our all out words of undertakings
That we have bestowed upon you
From all shore of human races
The Nobel prize of all our hearts.

(In memory of Mother-Teressa)

September 19, 1997
Long Island, New York

IN THE GUISE OF A FRIEND

Bengali: 'Bondhu Sheje'

(Frankka in vision)

You are a friend, whereas flooded with greed in your heart,
Squeezing the whole body of mine
Like the udder of a cow you want to suck out
All my nutritious life-strength.

Upon gotten cut my vein
The stream of blood that flows,
To satisfy your thirst you are anxious to the brim
To pour down that whole flow into your throat.

You know, that will finish me,
Whereas you pretend as guise of a friend
That, - it is nothing --
Only then, you will divide and grab my body
In the cover of coating of many scenarios of Upstream Farakka's
Designed contracts and it's sweet definitions.

You thought I would not know,
Would not understand your flawless deceitful strike,
I'm not a lost-mind nonunderstanding ruller-machine,
I'm a life-thriven vigilant guard of crores of voices, crores of
minds

September 23, 1997
Long Island, New York

Notes:
Farakka - The Farakka dam built by India off-shore of North-West of Bangladesh

LITTLE HUMAN

Bengali: 'Chutto Manob'

Beautiful dresses, orderly movements-
Some has heavy degrees
Some empty with degrees but stylish.

On the way comes high rise modern buildings, orderly
I moved away with politeness
By the side--,

From the dark hollowness of the space
like a shooting star, in the twinkling of an eye
Something has happened, -- Suddenly
From my side, collapsed
The modern buildings--,

created underground
A huge hole,
From inside of it came out
A little human, in hand a ribbon-lamp
The little light of the little human has lightened up the hole

December 6, 1997
Long Island, New York

GIVE ME A HUMAN

Bengali: 'Akti Manob Dao'

Give me a human
Whose aim would be one and undivided,
Who can not be tempted with sweet talks,
Always whose destination is resolute, and
The path of cirumbulation isn't under seize by mystique.

Give me that one human child
Whom tricky ferociousness or boisterous influence
Can not control,
Who does not take shelter under malice
Who can step over the network of corruptions.

Give me that human
Who have understood the wicked rules of the dreadful minds
Of politicians and have constructed his own principles,
Who will catch hold the roots of scandalous disgrace of
educational institutions
And drive them away in the oblivion.

Give me that one human
Whereupon, the broken heart burns in funeral pyre under the
thrush of demonic influence,
And whose only one single wish would subdue those,
And will result in the end of them
From the chest of this nation of hopeful buds.

Give me that brave lion human
Who knows how to love the unfortunates,
Have feelings for the oppressed, in the hearts of repressed
Can bring the tastes of perceiving the nectar of life
That all human he will lift to heart with love and affection,
Give me that very single human
To whom I will give another one hundred man
Collecting from every corner of the country
Who will take up the handle of fearlessness under his command,-
Because-
I'll take him to establish my rights,
As the only worthy ruller, director and a whole life-giving tool.

November 4, 1997
Long Island, New York

FACE TO FACE ON HARTAL

Bengali: 'Hartal-er Poyshala'

All the roads of the capital are empty, desolate
There are no vehicles, no gathering of people.
The same scenario in every city of the country.
Empty of people, Rickshaws also have taken goodbye.
To-day is Hartal, the same way it was lots of yesterdays, even
before that,
The political parties called for this Hartal
Not in the interest of the country but a bluffing game.

No wheels of cars are moving in the roads,
Fearful lest be assaulted and broken into pieces, perhaps--,
For, this comfort earned after lots of hard works...
The wheels of the well-to-do may not be on the road,
But no matter, the wheels of their stomach are not stopped,
Rickshaws, day laboureres, industry labours and their earning-
wheels
When stopped on the roads are also stopped at home in the endless
darkness

The people who call for this Hartal stay in divan
In comfort sofa, their wheels are not shut,
Roll non-stop, no worry for their stomach whereas no job either,
The name is politician, the big jobless job
Money comes non-stop, crores and crores..unlimited..
They have no pain in this earning, life is a dole for labours,

M. Hasan Imam

Low-middleclasses, for whom this Hartal gets success,
out of fear or no fear, their life is under seize.

The productivity of the whole country goes under dog,
The day by day earners count days of doom,
But the politician leaders keep high tones
That the Hartal does not harm the economy, the country,
Hartal for realizing demands they say! Ten pounds of milk
Must be gotten from this cow, if needed, be beaten to death, they deem-
The calf needn't be fed only collect milk,
Let the calf die..no harm.! These they want
to rule the land? for the betterment and progress of the country
We want fresh bloods who didn't get contagious, aren't corrupted,
Need their stepping in.

October 20, 1995
Port Washington, New York

Note:
Hartal = Strike with no vehicles on street, no shops open.

IN A RAINY DAY

Bengali: 'Bristi Jhora Diney'

To-day in this rainy morning-afternoon time
Boys and girls together are in playful exaltation
In this village courtyard up above of which is sky-touching clouds
Getting themselves wet in sweet bubbling and laughter.

To-day in this rainy morning-afternoon time
Mind runs towards the fields of childhood,
Come afloat in the vessel of memory, the playful
Moments and the words of unforgotten contentment.

To-day in this rainy morning-afternoon time
The memory moments of picking mangoes play around
In the gardens and distant forests of heart. All day,
Waterbathing and amusements sports playing in the house-pond.

To-day in this rainy morning-afternoon time
The craze-gone flowers at the site humming bees
Are resounding with joy and laughter; the swans of mind-buds
Wakes up in the distant shore of memory.

To-day in this rainy rhythmic joyous mements
The huddle of boys and girls are coming out in a glee
Waking up, the world cries in silent sorrows
Upon disappointments of being unable to go back in old days.

June 1, 1971
Hajigonj, Comilla

A FLOOD OF LOVE

Bengali: 'Ek Bonna Prem'

This is life! Sometimes torned apart, Sometimes detached,
Sometimes spreading the aroma of rose petals all around
You make the conflicting stunned divine grace of creation
More deeper, more clearer.

The deeds of your life, the affection and touch
Of your love, and the sharpeness of your look
Tie me in bathe in compound of love,
By spreading the wings of white swan, as if,
Make me drown and float, and cover my whole
In pervently overflowing songs of rhythm
In unsubdued deep desire of touch like the intense attraction of
Lover's lips. This heart, I know,
This reinless horse of love and amity will run
In that endless horizon only, for once,
To be carried away into the stars of your eyes;
Of all the sleepless nights, like the anxious dreams
That come round and around, stumbling
For once in the courtyard of the shore of your love,
It will come running in joy and sorrow
In the midst of this heart.

At that moment, in that blind attraction moment
Like the shooting stars, would you, in the corner of your heart
Note down a verse, only a prayer
Hey love beauty! my, this wreath of perseverance,

Braving the forest under heavy obstacles of desert storms
I knitted and brought in the warm fountain of your love
In dying secret into your lap.

That day from the chained-mind of jail
The letter I wrote to you, with the beads of humble prayers
Of my mind the garland that
I have decorated in absolute closeness;
In each knots of countless desire of each bead
The throbbing heart that lighted up with sparkles,
In the vast sky of sea of hope the pulsatory heart
That ran into the crowed of countless stars in search of you,
That hope of heart as songs of pain and sorrow
Came back in deep solitude; In your
spell-bound-self in your eye-lid nectar
The bird of my heart, that day, couldn't get sprinkled,
The flesh and blood peacock of my awaitedness
Couldn't get bathied by spreading the dream-wings
In your love garden.

The then, you were in meditation in unornamental captivation
In pellucid flooded quietness of moonlit night, you were in ascetic
austerities-
Deep in immerse in your wavy-beauty's lusting thirst,
That's why, besides an exchange of moment's look, that day,
In your beautiful enchanting eyes, this me,
An unrestrained free bird of flooded-love
couldn't pick you up in my wings,
Couldn't pick up my life long gift of nourishing love
The only things that's due to me.

You know I love you,
The mighty ray of the sun can't even
Burn that love from a very close proximity;
In the sky, with cloud's murmering

The dance of peacock you have seen,
I'm the rhythmic speed of that dance at your sight.
With a thrilling ignited sensation I, like a skilled dancing star
Run to your courtyard with a hope to get you!

In the past, so many times, your deep absorption to yourself
Has made you-
The slow pace hidden magic influence,
It has made you the divine grace of all hearts.
Like the look that remains hidden in your mystique essence of
shyness
You have conquered the thirst of all ambitions.
But this overwhelmed me, from that look of illusion
Still couldn't pick up the pearl,
Even now, that dream-blanket from the captivation of the past
Drown my whole mind and body in a festivity of hope.

To-day, in search of honey from this torned rose petal
Me, the bee, came into this free arena in your courtyard,
Breaking the jail door, to-day, I have come
To pick up that garland of comforting unattained devotion
Into my preserved heart that soaked to the brim with adorned
love!
The heart that was full of fire, full of innumerable
Unhappy buds of sorrows for not getting you,

Once the vessel of accumulated love,
To-day that will again be flooded with love
Unbounded aroma of spell-bound, ottor, roses
You and me loving in a flood of love.

June 19, 1981
Hotel Metropolitan
Dhaka, Bangladesh

ALLOW TO GO FORWARD

Bengali: 'Agote Dao'

Let me forget, Hey! Great Heart
The regrets of all things done in the past
If, by doing mistakes--
I have suffered the prices of those mistakes, then-
Give me relief in this present
Colorful morning of the day.

Give me strength and courage to forget that mistake
To go forward
In the new morning--,
let me build my mind
With new vigor, --to win again
Your gifts in the struggles of life.

I forget by force
Bringing back the mind towards the future,
Still, why the memory of mistakes
Come back again and again to torment this mind.
Even going far away, suddenly it appears at the present
Unnoticed in the corner of the mind,
It peeps, - I should have thought to it this way, that way
In the sea of your kindness give me relief from this mental agony.

January 9, 1998
Port Washington, New York

TOUCHING LIFE
LITTLE BY LITTLE

Bengali: 'Gibonkay Chuey Chuey'

The indomitable dance of storm
Don't need, -- the fearful thunderbolt
Assuming a full form.

The mighty violent tidal bore from the sea
And it's frightening roar
Murmuring and destroying rushing to the shore,

Thirty forty feet high turbulent intense waves
From the heart of the sea
Coming up engulping the shore

All of these are not needed to prove the almightiness of yours
Even without such frightening forms,
The wonder of your power is amazingly wonderful

A sudden appearance of thick fog while passing the road
Your this supernatural little ingredient
Could cover and diminish under the fog--

The well-alive busy working lives of this world,
Could seize and bring to stand-still
The lively moments of all lives.

Even a little more denser fog
Could bring to end this
Living planet with just a touch of your mightyness.

You are kind, you're great the mighty of almighty
That's why you let this life-lamp know with little by little touch
Your existence presence and the gift of your nobleness.

January 9, 1998
Port Washington
Long Island, New York

STRIKE

Bengali: 'Ughut'

I know, it is not your liking
That I write poems--
Your resistance doesn't listen forbidding
To stop the source of my rhythm.

Whether you think or don't think
Just by wishing,- the poems
Can not be stopped,
Whether you want or don't want
Just by wishing, - the talk of living (life) of the people
Can not be stopped nor be caged.

I, in the interest of people's minimum standard of living,
In their favour, want only to uphold
The picture of humanity, --
So many political and social abominable practices
Have seized by the neck of this weak human,
Squeezing them day in day out incessantly
Beyond the geographical area here and there
In land, in other lands, underdeveloped & developed lands alike.

Still you have objections!
You think what's the use in this spoiling of time!
But you didn't think
Of a very small point--,

Repression of the strong upon the weak
The corrupted forceful authority of the law
Didn't penetrate and got rooted in one day,

Day by day, the wrong foundation that
Has entrenched into this human society in the guise of 'right',
It will take time to break it as well.
Got to continue writing through strong message of poems
Without thinking it to be wastage of time,
You got to break the chains of wrong attachments
Day by day striking little by little.

September 16, 1997
Long Island, New York

NONETHELESS, YOU CAME

Bengali: 'Tobu Tumi Ashechilley'
(In memory of Mother Teresa)

Your wanderous world now, is,
In an extra-mundane celestrial environment beyond human
knowledge,
Created by God's own hand
In overwhelmed eternal garden of sweet aroma.

The fever-sicks, troubled with sorrows and misery of this bank
The befallen sickly distressed lives that lie on the roads
Hungry, neglected, the bony bodies
Have become deprived from your affectionate motherly touch
For ever--.

For so long, these unfortunate mourning souls
Having enjoyed the care, affection and nursing of your motherhood
Have engaged themselves, out of habits, in a remorse hope
That, without you, even two moments wouldn't do.
That we have got to loose you
The simple open minds of these afflicted healths
Didn't think a moment of this unforgivable truth.

Nevertheless, you came--
Loved these neglected human
You have given the full moonlit love
The body and mind of your whole existence throughout your life.

Nonetheless, you have touched these
Suffering souls, ill miseried leprosy's hands,
Have given them consolations,
The taste of life of a human being.

Nonetheless, you have come--
Sat next to them holding their hands,
Picked them up in your lap,
Have given in the ear to ear of hearts
The attachment of hearts--
Have commended, witnessing the human sufferings-
I leave behind with my nursing tearful heart
The salvation of human,
That's why you are the life mother of world's suffered humanity.

Nevertheless, you came--
Irrespective of caste creed and color
With the blessings of God
At our shore--
We submit to that in tearful eyes
And we are blessed.

(In memory of Mother Teresa)

September 13, 1997
Long Island, New York

I PROFOUNDLY LOVE THIS TWIN-PONDS BANK

Bengali:
'Borro Valobashi Ai Zorra Pookur Dhar'

The morning awakening call comes from the ducks-hens house
Ku-Kuruk-Ku, in my village home.
Pretty soon, the resounding of closed one's would come rise
The sound of AJAN in-tune came to an end a while ago.

The golden luster of the sun have spread all over the east
Announcing the end of the dark; The big courtyard of the house
Needs to be passed to go to the outer house and the
Sounds of foots are clearer now; the rests are awakening slowly.
The big two ponds in the middle of which

The connection-yard to walk & use. In the Ghut of south side pond
The well-known kith and kins are busy washing hands and faces,
Ahead of these twin-ponds is the Main-gate,
Passing that innerway is the Mosque, next to it is the Majlishkhna,
Adjacent to its is the Kacharighor; surrounding these the young &
old alike

Are exchanging slight talks, little smile in the morning light,
The whole body and mind of oneself isn't fully awake yet,
Some having little conversation in between tooth brushing,
Some are ready to step into the Ghut-

Just waiting for the other one to vacate the spot,
Some are little hesitant
In the face of the olders as a guesture of respect.

The North side pond, in day to day life
Is used mostly by the innercircle of the house; in the outer side-
It's use isn't being practiced, the Ghut wasn't placed either,
Why, - is not known, may be because
It wasn't just used; In the middle of these friendly talks
And coming & going of the relative folks,
The soft red glow of sun is almost gone. In the house,
After finishing the breakfast with Muri some are heading to paddy-
fields,
The younger ones sat in study in Kacharighor infront of the
Master,
Some are ready to go to job.

The wives are busy arranging needy things in the house,
Stepping forward to readying every one; the sun is rising high
In the horizon, the diamond drops in the body of paddys
Are gone by now, the butterfly flying, insects ad beetles
Are showing up with two three small Shalik-birds in the
surroundings.

In the cheek of Durbaghus the wet feelings now
Has taken dry hard feeling, life is on the move
Through the change of every step, later in the way
To fulfillment towards the marblestone of hope & aspirations.
In a forign land-
Sitting in it's cruel quietness, a constant thought overcomes,- I
love
Profoundly love the bank shades of that twin-ponds of my childhood
And it's surrounding still like before.

July 4, 1995
Long Island, New York

Notes:

Ajan- The loud recitation for Quran as Muslim's call for prayer
at prayer time.

Ghut- Landing stage/steps of pond

Mosque- Sacred house of Allah (Muslim's prayer house)

Majlishkkhana- A sitting room/house for guests or meetings

Macharighor- Study room built for kinds & housing fo
Masters.

Master - A tutor kept for teaching.

Muri - Kind of cerealbmade of rice.

Shalik - Small birds of a kind

Durbaghush - Very solf slowgrowing grass but turdy to sustain life.

NEW NATION FROM BENEATH THE EARTH

Bengali: 'Vugorvo Theke Notton Desh'

The country isn't big in terms of square miles,
In terms of visibility of general life
It is very big, located by the coast of Bay of Bengal,
Full of vast human habitation
It is filled in every corner,
That's my Ma, my motherland-
The dwelling place of my childhood & the restlessness of my
adolescence,
The heart of heart of my youth my dearest mother,
In her affection filled heart, the fascinating

Attraction of green waves, full of dark-blue-green colour
Illusions all over-. I am a student.
Book at hand sitting at the verandah of my house,
My father is planting the baby fruit tree
Into the ground with great care
Beneath the soil of hope In this hand
Firmly held is the tool
To unfold the ground which is as penetrating as my pen
That I held in my hand, just

Like the bubbling hope of moment's before
The blossoming of the buds in the flower-plant of the garden.

Those beautifully arranged flower plants
Planted by my father are awakening

In favour of solemnity in a way that shows
In courtyards of every huts in Bangladesh.
It has lots of population but doesn't matter; In the pocket
underneath the earth
There are deposits of hearts like the promise of firmly held.
Tool as it is in my father's hand.

In the crops field cultivation with plough is on the go,
In the middle of two bulls, the plough that's connected to their
shoulders
Come down to the edge of wood at the hand of farmer
Who pushes it down beneath the ground,
The soil breaks apart in two sides
As the bulls pull & walk,
The ground is being readied worth for cultivation,
Like that of same hope in the garden
Moments before blossoming of buds-

Peep through the minds of farmers,
In the hands of Ana Mia the same tune
Is surely commissioned with great strength of the plough
He doesn't allow it to be a failure-
My father's devoted employee, he is full of
Supervising & responsibility sense who
Look after the family farm-lands with pride.
In the silent flow of quiet air of the morning,
In the green paddy field

The wave rises, in the chest of farmers
The thrill dances, becomes filled with touch of
Pure pleasure, Even though, the complete three meals
May not be there always in the house, the reaping of this pleasure,
As if, is not to be missed; The hope surfaces

In the awaiting chests surrounding the evening.
This is the land of farmers, fertile to conceive,
The country to aspire crops of cultivated lands.
This sky that holds breath of twelve crores people
Have contained the people's affection into kinship,
There is no wealth in every sphere, there still, is
Touch of fellow feelings for the neighbour, to other people, to the
unknown;
Like the fertility of farm-lands, this lofty
richness of people's heart has envied the foreigners,
And surprised them. Having so so little,
This people has seemingly built the mountain of self-contenment,
and
Have actually culminated & portrayed in the map of the world

A heavenly beam that shines in the minds of foreigners
To see so little demand of this people!
Surrounded by fifty four thousand square miles
The hope of this people is at the gulp of hope.
One day, from underneath the Bay of Bengal,
Like the message of God being engraved,
With the sparkles of fire into the chest of mountain, when
A land like Bangladesh would rise touching chottrola, hatiia,
shondip-

Adhering to the mainland, --then
Hey! human lover Great Heart-
You caution the greed of other nations,
Let them not to held fire in their eyes to see outcome of others,-
Because, this newly arised land belongs to this people
Who has given the world curiosity
By showing unbelievable contentment of possessing so little,
Their demand is limited but
The core of heart is vastly spread that which they will bear
In this new land combining the old.

I see, sitting down, with the pen in my hand,
The sharp spade, axes are stronger
Because of the vigilance of the joined lands,
Like the plghhanble in powerful hand of the farmer.
The speed of my pen is heading into a definitive path
To that plough, the soil is uprooted, falling apart in two sides

With a hope for the seeds to conceive,
The axe is visible over the head held in two hands,
Will cut into pieces the strong body of trees taken down,
The cut wood pieces would file up with hard labour,
The burned wood fire would give blessings to this joined land as,
'The New Nation - in this fashion like
Putting the crown on the head of farmer, so saying -
I am thankful to have met -
Your contenment, your heavenly sight,
Bravo to your austerity, to your intentness.

March 13, 1996
Port Washington, New York

Notes: Hatia, Shondip, chottrola -- Islands of Bangladesh.

THIS IS NOT MY END

Bengali: 'A Nohe Mur Shomapti'

I din not want to remain only as poet,
The variety of vibrating essence of flower-garlands
Will distract my invigorating buds of aspirations!
This is not the end of my work desire.
The millions of clappings of yours would let sink
My ability to save the oppressed humanity
This is not the end of acquirement of my life.

The endless praises and thousands of colums
Accumulating on my desk in tens of monds, - and
That will submerge me under the hip of papers!
Kindling the light of hope of destitute boys, youths
The befallen misery and eclipsed paw of politicians upon society,
I'll uproot
This desire of mine will sink under the melee of praises.
This is not the end of thorough manifestation of my hope.

November 10, 1995
Long Island, New York

FADING OF EUPHORIA

Bengali: 'Euphoriar Oboshan'

Now, euphoria is somewhat, as if,
Under the power-influence of tranquilizer,
Descending in the runway of factual reality.
After the end of travels, the dreamy nerves
Are taking time, --slowly,
The surroundings are awakening in front of eyes
With liveliness and individual identity.

The news of political torture in the page of News Papers
Are spreading out the awakening sounds of Wolfs,
Here, the wild forest-dogs and hyenas
Don't differ much, -- only
The foxes, in disguise of petty dogs, in the courtyard of helpless people
Are snipping through the nose all the time,
In the house is the groaning of the hungry---.

In this week, the rent has to be paid, the school fees of the son,
The outer-house dress of the daughter, -- after that
A full pledged check to pay-off loan instalments,
Milk for the younger child and the last capricious request of the
wife,

Euphoria is now swirling in the whirling fumes of reality,
Finding some means, it wants to flee away,
Without looking at the electric bills,
The telephone math is, of course, yet to be mentioned!

The land has to be ploughed,-- the twin bulls are all boney
Like the owner farmer--
Plough will still be tied on their shoulders,
The land will be turned suitable for cultivation--
The green paddy leaves will swing in the free air
Like a cool comforting touch to the eyes,
The farmer will harvest golden paddy crop in dreamy illusion
A new hope gets life in the old breath.

The hope, that euphoria was indulging, breaks apart after a while,
The value of harvesting doesn't satisfy the expenses of cultivation,
The family falls short in cash--,
The daily family expenses, -- where is the income!
And the expenses of the son in the rural town!
Thought engulfed the boney driver of the boney bulls in the field.

Days come and go, only pain remains
When, the much heard of developments, will anchor in this shore?

January 3, 1996
Manor Sands Pharmacy
Port Washington, New York

STILL A VAIN MOCKERY
OF VICTORY

Bengali:
'Akhono Bejoer Bartho Porihush'

Still the victory day comes like before
Only the radiance of victory is of lifeless soundless step,
Yes, arrived vivid political torture, scenes of Hartals
Upon the chest of general populace is a raid of muddy dirt in liberty

They, only, indulge in politics of how to occupy the throne
In the name of demands for general people, ignite tickling,
They, only, plot schemes to keep occupying the throne
By spreading the ledger of developments in the face of the hungry,
The majority niety percent people who are being whipped with
claimed developments
Are drowning boney under worser conditions than before.

Still the victory day comes like before
It's name is victory, the increased fortune of countable few
Still the deliverance of victory is only distorted revelation
For the welfare of human it's a divulgation of utter failure of on-
going politics.

November 30, 1995
Port Washington, New York

Notes: Hartal - It's a day called by political parties to stop every acts of business and transport in a country and cities.

WHEN I WILL GO BACK

Bengali: 'Jokhon Firey Jubo'

When I'll go back in the lap of my dear motherland
In an untiring late afternoon--,
While was at abroad
Many buds of affectionate attachments have dropped death then.
The elder dear relatives
Bearing an eternal pain into their chest for not being able to see me
Have taken leave in silent,
The afflicted needle-pinched mind bee of uncontent hopes
Have fallen down breathless at eternity's call.

From the light of experiences and affections of the elders
This heart is deprived for so long,
And the suppressed murmuring of self-cry would burst in silence
all time
But nobody would know--
The nearest dear ones living next to my body
Wouldn't even hear that humming sound of sorrow and pain for
lost ones,
Like, surrounded in all sides in the hidden hole of dusk
The way the sorrows of the darkness get blended.
Only, one or two blinking stars
Will peep into that very place
Quietly at the bottom of the hole.

When, I'll go back in the lap of my dear motherland,
The 'Dheul', 'Gughu' of the then known courtyard
I may not see flying in their youthful play-vigor,
After waiting for so long
For this dear good friend
They may be gone at unknown destiny,
Only this me, will count the days again
To get back the play home of old time
In my own self.

October 3, 1996
Port Washington, New York

Notes:
Dheul - the singing bird
Ghughu - A bird of pigeon size common bird back home

HUMANITY DETACHED FROM THE STALK SLOWLY COMING DOWN

Bengali: 'Numchey Dheray Brintocchuto Munobota'

I see snow storm falling down from the sky
Like a dream of eternal fountain,
Sometimes it's like cotton
Sometimes Woolen grain,
It does not appear that the sky has broken apart, --only
Floating and falling non-stop,

Suddenly gets speed by the slap of the wind-
Solemn nature all around,
As if the aberration of humanity
Coming down detaching from the stalk, thereafter
Lying on the body of ground or like coral hill.

Strongly held in the clutch of my three fingers
My pen and from it's spine
Blue blood like running arrow
Aimed through the air, - then
In the paper
Getting alliance in composing words.

In Search Of Light

I see snow storm-
Like humanity slipping through the body of civilized sky in Bosnia.
In different habitations of Africa
Here and there in the Middle East, in Chechnia

In the poor areas of underdeveloped and developing nations of Asia,
Worldwide in the black, brown and white's
Unhealthy living homes of slums,
And country after country refined political torture
Upon the chest of general populace.

I see snow is falling-
The definitions of human values are closing shut and
Scattering around in front of my eyes,
Filing hills of snows, inches, feets and even more
Foots are measuring upwards,
Ridiculing the developments of civilization,
Scattered human races
With no foods, hungry, half-fed, taking the tastes of malnutrition
as they live
Without treatments pass weeks months
Like the snow fall in scattered flash of beam.

Snow is falling defeating fifty years of history
The January of Nineteen Ninety Six
Has broken all the records
Like cottons in the guise of snow flakes,
For the committed welfare of all humans, the degraded inches of
humanity
Is growing up, as though,
Like the snow fall, all over the world.
Developments of civilization should be alike
For all human beings
Like it is in the palaces of wealthy and well to-do
Unto the hungry homes and habitations of the poor & unfortunates.

I see snow falls detaching from the stalk of humanity dripping
down the tormented steps
And filling up around me,
Experienced strikes of the crowbar
Making it file up high here and there disregarding the general rules
Like the shots from destructive cannons,
The weariness of deprived and neglected humanity still
Filling up in the old places
Only to draw attention of proclaimed civilization
In the hope of getting a little touch of mercy and affection.

January 17, 1996
Port Washington, New York

IN THE FIELD OF KONOK TARA

Bengali: 'Konok Turer Khate'

The wave is playing in the field of Konok Tara
The pride of the farmer swings
With thy rhythm of the wave into the tingling air.

The paddy Konok Tara getting mixed with green leaves
And spreading a golden glow
In the captivated attachment of the high land.

In the fallen sun with rosy cheeks
Ulta in the foots, the farmer girl
Walks in the light-vibrating rhythm of Nupoor.

The borders of Konok Tara field, as if,
Laughs with new life at dusk
In mind-stealing rhythmic sound of Nupoor.

In the Boroi tree at the high bank of the field
Green, orange and yellow colours are blended in
The fruits and are politely welcoming the visitors.

Be careful to go under the Boroi tree
Chances are to get picked with thorns of fallen little branches
It's fruits are sweet and sour mixed.

With the help of the paddy harvesting sickle
The farm worker scratches his itchy back
Holding the graspful of cut paddy in his hand.

He stands up to straighten the backbone
Many a times leaning down with sickle in hand
They start singing in chorus the paddy cutting songs.

At day end, after finishing the cutting of paddy plants
They tie up bundles of paddy in big bunches,
Put them on top of head & start transporting home.

Not once, not twice
As many as dozen times, bunches on top of head
They make up and down trips to home.

In the evening after finishing dinner in moonlit night
They start thrashing paddy singing melodious songs
By walking bulls encircling a pole in house's courtyard.

April 13, 1993
Port Washington, New York

Notes:
Nupoor - Anklets with small bells
Ulta - Decorating red color for feet and hands.
Konok Tara - Flavourus long grain/Name.
Boroi - A kind of tropical fruits

WEAK THAT HELPLESS

Bengali: 'Durbol Jay Oshohai'

Nobody wants to leave them
Unhurt, - at least anybody, he she or they
Like a raft floating away in Monsoon
Are their lives---,

A bunch of bodies of banana trees
Tied together to make their raft, - or
A bundle of bamboo trees tied together as raft, ---
Their lives float on it
In the swing of life-,

May not be utterly penniless but helpless in city, villages
In the face of rude attitude of
Local or Moholla bandits -
Their backbone is unwilling to be strong-, 'Cause
There is no supporting strength behind them,
So, remain weak
This mind and body-,

The life of weak and helpless
The worth of keeping alive
Society will make it understand, - where?

Another picture wakes up
In the brush scratch of the artist,

This people is helpless
Still wants to have peace-
In this own corner in his own sphere
Not in any ones door, not doing harm to any one,
Keeping busy in silent by himself,

This hope of the weak and helpless
The prayer to be spared
The society will make it understand, - Why not!

December 11, 1997
Port Washington, New York

UPON IRREGULARITY AND NEGLECT

Bengali: 'Oniom Obohelai'

It is too much of irregularities
In a regularized calendar,
The ingredients of sustaining your life
The flow of water-nectar in a timely fashion
Was not followed for a long time.

Leaves, arms are dropping off your body
Giving the signal of untimely loss,
The hardship of life in pulling with difficulty
The soundless revolt
Are bringing clear sign of pain.

In the soft green comfortable body
The caress touch of hand, whereupon,
Would have given pleasure,
Now, in an inopportune time, due to neglected crossing of
regularity
It's distress body is dropping infront of eyes.

Who knows for how deep displeasure reasons
This dropping of your body suffers,
How much illness, malnutrition and unknown sufferings
Renders your body breaking apart

Slipping bit by bit, leaves after leaves.
(Farakka in vision)

January 22, 1998
Port Washington, New York

Note: Farakka - The dam built by India that ruined Bangladesh

ARE YOU THAT FREEDOM

Bengali: 'Tumiei Ki Sheie Shudhinota'

So many days and nights passed, ceaseless anxiety
Year after year slipped by in darkness sleep,
Posh, Mugh also bid goodbye in the heat of Choitra, still-
Hei liberty, I couldn't yet know you.
This is my misfortune Hei Freedom, - whom
By holding in the crown, this bullet pierced heart
Wanted to have it dearly at home; - For whom the
Shameful deaths were accepted cordially in heart by the
Virgin women, the teen aged adolescents, - are you that liberty?

You are liberty, - that's what I hear in my
Surroundings, - From the quarrely vultures-
In the dead flashes of cattles which are being fighted upon
To be snatched and divided; - The apprehension of death is
dreadful
Hei Freedom, I have accepted that to wear you
In my crown, that also went dim,
That's why it comes to mind-
Where are you, Freedom? - From the fearful apprehension of death
The smell of death is yet more frightening,
Very much lifeless like a stone speechless, as if,
To get frozen and I made that mine too
Hei liberty, - only because I would take you
To make my crown. In my ear, day after day
In silence, in solitation the wounded air keeps murmering

M. Hasan Imam

That you are not that Freedom, that Liberty ---!
Then who are you? The messenger of my dream is bulleted
In hundreds of thousands of porous wounds and afflicted, the way
In tremendous storms the swirling straw keeps whirling,
Why you are destroying like that for no reason, in destructive
stream-!

In your chest, my real motherland, - with this claim
I'll walk around, with that aspirations by the lap of
Hajigonj town in the heart of Dakatia river-
Have be fallen dead on enemy assailent's bullets, many many
Innocents sons of Bengal; Holding you tight
In my chest, with Freedom..Freedom shouts I'll send out
Tremulous Shivering Voice, - with this thunderous promise
Many golden faces of Bengal lie down
In the lap of that Dakatia with hands and feets tied behind
And faces spreaded with poisonous acids by the enemy,
An untimely end of lives, their parents gifts,
The beloved lives, - only Hei Freedom--
To hold you in the crown.

Thousands of Dakatia river like this one, we ran through
With no foods no clothes no proper education,
Have only life to sacrifice to lay down with a promise
To conquere only to get little peace surrounding you,
A very little fruit of life we will get, with this
Hope Hei Liberty-, we have embraced
The terrible strike of bayonets into this heart,
Holding you high in the grip we ran
In the road, in the horizon; But alas! What happened, - say,
Say it with solmn sworning, are you
That Freedom? - Whom I have given birth
In my dreams in reality with a hope for Liberty!

That I'll wear you as my crown, for that matter
I have fallen down upon thousands of bayonet charges
In rows of thousands of massacres, genocides, - Still

I am alive - and,
didn't loose my own identity's
Directives, - Hei Liberty, are you that?

Holding you tight into my bossom I'll
Build the dwelling of hope, for that cause, Hei Freedom,-
Hundreds of miles I walked through, - shoeless, waering Lungi,
Half pants tinted with dirts, clays,
In dark bunkers, in boats,
In marsh and swamps, in paddy fields,
In lined up shades of jute-fields, aligning to the shore of
Monsoon next to Denga of village houses, Hiding-
By the high bank of ponds, and coming out quietly from
the shades of water-hycinths into the main roads,
I have clasped the Three-Knot songs of death, Hei Freedom-
Only hope that I'll make you my crown dearly!
Tell.. Tell me to-day, time has passed
In fruitless sorrows, tell-
Are you the same dear Liberty of mine!

All around me, I hear to-day weeping and wailing
Lamentations; Breaking apart the chest, the songs of blood stream
Are shedding tears; yelling Liberty- Liberty
Like the throbbing of blood in the mouth
Spreading around as foam carelessly in adverse indifference,
Tell..tell me Hei Freedom -
Are you the same dear Liberty of mine!

February 10, 1996
Port Washington, New York

Notes:
Poush, Mugh, Choitro- These are names of Bengali months.
Lungi - A common people's dress
Denga - Outskirts of village home
Three-Knots - Name of rifle

BE STAND UP IN MY ROW

Bengali: 'Daria Jeo Amar Katare'

If   Suddenly at the impact of harsh brush-sound
           The blood from my chest stream around
           In the public thoroughfare, in Mohollas in lanes
           Rolling at the feets of crores of subdued Closed hands
           Oppressed hungry people,

If   At any instant moment, it gets closed
           All the things that were built by this hand
           The work-projects of plans beneficial to mankind,
           In the slipped off human villa who faints in wailing griefs,

Then   Forgive me-
           In the steaming eye drops of memory
           At bare hands,
           Things that meant to be completed, the work fields that
           Meant to wipe away hunger
           That I couldn't finish thus don't allow
           Regret to overwhelm
           Be stand up with those responsibilities
           In my duty row that I have left behind.

March 20, 1997
Port Washington, New York

COLOR DIFFERENTIALS WAKES UP UNDER OBSESSION

Bengali: 'Obsessionay Jaggay Utthay Borno Boishommo'

I thought, sitting in the intimate womb of civilized world
I'll pass the time, the thought of clash among human then
Will bid goodbye in the oblivion.

All around is only prologue of amity
Fragrances of Otto, roses resounding in the air,
the skin color, - it's horror and remorse
Will fade away from the melee of the society,

The merriments of civilization in the air all over
By the rights, by the left, in the back of human,
In the corner here and there of social groups,
Distracted exultations and summations of expressions every where,
But the revolting strike of color still
Did not fade away,
Division wakes up in the human shore
With all hopes and aspirations and their fulfillments though being \
achieved
In the sitting shore of these proud civilizations.

The capable and famous American Foot-baller O.J. Simpson
implicated
Double murder case becomes monstrous looking
In every nerve of the society
In the unadulterated tide of all human
In the court, in the published photos & in the media excited
magnetic reports,
The pierced impression of skin color carry away
The equality and balance of opinions in the wooden box of justice.

T.V. and News Media's unworthy
Excessively implied meaningless importance of war-trumpet
Tore off the silent cover of skin color differentials.
T.V. robs rates.
Human gets hunger of hyenas!

The activities of social values, welfare, the hot news of Clinton
Administration
Get sunk throughout the Country the year round,
Awake only O.J. Simpson in every way.

Imposed by the media on the neck of society
The blind addicted disarray impassionate outburst of human
Run after Nicole Simpson, Ronald Goldman and
O.J. Simpson's case under seize of obsession.

An incorporeal voice echoes in the air
Is media for human, or
human is for the media
Time has come to think over.

April 16, 1997
Long Island, New York

CREATION IN THE TRAP OF CREATION

Bengali: 'Sristir Kobolay Sristi'

Of all the creations one eats up the other
And survive, is that what we see?
This seems to be the normal, this is the nature.

One's life and the other's death
One creation is for the other-,
All the 'selfs' has it's own place
For some ages, for some time
For continuous spending-,
Thereafter the scenary of end.

There is no end of God's graces
And there is no end of the sea of knowledge,
At His will one's life and sacrifices
Dedicated in other's path of walk
Other's path of survival,
Life and death is within this definite time of compliance-
In the endless cycle of creation this is the firm tie.

The small tiny fish in the corner of the pond
Bet the life
With the mighty clever Boal fish,
Deers of the forests likewise

Keep alive, goes into stomach of tigers, lions at their strike,
The sharks at the sea pick up plenty of prey
At the bottom of it's world in cool touch,
The birds pick up insects, flies in it's beak in he shade of forests.

In all these play houses of this life
The hunter survives and the prey survives as well
Only the number remains in maintaining harmony,
Under the umbrella of infinite rules of the creator
The human race isn't different too-,
In the cycle of creations, they also survive, kill and eat
Their name, though, stays in the book as the greatest of all
creations.

November 21, 1997
Port Washington, New York

Notes:
Boal fish- Name of a tropical big fish with big mouth.

LET ME THINK A WHILE OKLAHOMA

Bengali: 'Umake Aktu Vubte Deo Oklahoma'

Give me a heart to be able to reach at the
Core of human feelings; For what curseful aspirations
The lively lives in the world
Are being ruined-dead to the dust, the God's own-hand made humans.
Your dirty hands of mixed dreadful knowledge of science
Have snatched away the hope of human house,
The chapter page of austere endevourer for welfare of others.
Even a child wasn't spared, who, sitting in
Three wheeled baby-cycle used to roam around
The neighbour's gardens in pleasureful stream.

In the arms of fireman, the bloodied body
That went dead-ruined is of that child,
The heap of fallen crumble building of Oklahoma
Removed carefully by the strike of shovels of the volunteers
That which salvaged this child's body
From the middle of the ruins of teddy-bear, dolls and others.
Suddenly from nowhere a wretched human of sickeny ill heart,
In the desire of ill-connection of senses has snatched away
Countless more childs, youth, adolescents, young and old
From the love of love ones of this world's dear courtyard.

M. Hasan Imam

Please, let me think a while-
To-day, from this vessel of grief, the potion-wine
Pour into my drunk body,
Pour into my throat all the exiled pains of human soul,
With one gulp let me swallow it at the bottom lava of my stomach.
Thereafter, let it come alive in painless new hope of life
At the shore of those our snatched away lives
Transforming into dear ones into the model anecdote of the
society.

Let me understand a little, let me reach --
At the core of human-mind feelings, where the songs of life
Are dead-- stopped at those heap of ruins; in their background
Whose humming sounds fill this courtyard! What you have
gained
In this uprooted lava of total ruins!?
Only this is my querry from the oppression of pain.

There peep a hope in the broken heart-
Again in the spring in this chest of lava the buds will bloom,
A new life, blossomed flowers
Shore up in the grief-filled warmth of past memory!

(In memory of lives lost in Oklahoma Federal building bombing)

April 20, 1996
Port Washington, New York

NOW AT SLEEP THE BEAUTIFUL PARAKEET

Bengali: 'Akhon Ghumonto Shundor Parakeet'

So small a bird whom in the palm of a hand
Could be retained in playful pleasure,
So small a life whom in the palm of a hand
Could be held in the name of act of play,
So small a body whom in the palm of a hand
Could be covered completely in the lap of hide and seek.
Green in colour awake all time in the myth of life,
In the cage all different kinds of acrobatic activities
Excite a silent pleasure in the skilled play house of nature.

That all these good feelings, love and sinless pleasure
In this toy-play of nature gives an impeccable flow of heart,
Suddenly, the bird is dyingly-sick and the pleasure kingdom falls
in pin drop silence
Held in hand the lifeless body of a life-full heart
The fruitless prayer of passionate outburst that this has to be saved,
Has to be kept alive this beautiful life that held in hand.
So small a body, it seems, anything could be done,
This is so nothing, whereas helpless human with all it's wisdom
Goes head-down in mental agony into the palm's lifeless beauty.

M. Hasan Imam

January 26, 1993
Port Washington, New York

Note:
Parakeet - A kind of bird

KEEPING BETTING

Bengali: 'Baje Rekhe'

I,too, was there for ages
One foot still lays -
There, to engrave the pain of it into my feelings.

Counting the days
They are heading in unending bravery
Betting their lives
Towards a vast empty sphere of uncertainty.

Not a fulfillment
Rather a struggle with their lives
Only this day this moment
Keep surviving for stepping into to-morrows doors.

Many a times
They have no worry at all
To safeguard noticeable anything
No need indeed specially since there's nothing to safeguard.

They who have some very little accessories,
With the strike of time
It's their day long worry and struggle to keephold that little
something
Only to pass days like those who don't have anything at all.

M. Hasan Imam

Many many people
Of this world
Walk around like human beings
Betting every drop of blood of their life.

November 19, 1997
Long Island, New York

MERGING TIME

Bengali: 'Akivuto Shomoy'

Merging time is in roll now
One in collaboration with another,
Names of getting amalgamated is growing high.

from center to bigger center
From big corporated institution,
Because of adding up, grow even bigger institutions,
Small, even smaller those that exist in places,
They experience shiver
At the fear of loosing existence.

Now, to be merged
Is the hot time running,
The bigger wants to swallow
The free life of the smaller ones,
That's why they lay out traps, or
Bring proposal outright
Invitation to get blended in their body.

The smaller ones get blended
In the spirit of merging-
It's a melee all around
As if the celebration of getting blandished.

The state and the greater interest of all populace
This merging in the long run whether would serve is yet to be seen.
Now, the time is at zero level to be merged
Whereupon, they who are hungry, unfed
Who are oppressed repressed under the traps of injustices
Throughout the time of humanity the burden of exulted sorrows
and griefs
Their uproar of their hearts-to-be-merged and aroused
Are still asleep and absent
From this very moments of unific-merging.

June 5, 1999
Port Washington
Long Island, N.Y.

ALL THESE TIMES, SIMPLY

Bengali: 'Atodin Shuddu'

All these days I simply have spoken
With the paper,
The pen has continued in its ink marking
Have sowed the garland of words,
The impatient swan opened its wings
And have spread widely
The sound of emotional recitation
With the quite clattering of words
Have spread artistries like the design in 'Nokshi Katha',
The glittering hopes have spread wings
Throughout the horizon
Filling page after page,

I am the poet and have spoken words
You are the paper, to you
Day and night along-
The running horse of civilization
Which I have stopped again and again
In this path, in the path of humans filled with tearful eyes,

Paper, I urged you
Don't let it go in utter delirium
Leaving behind the majority humans
Who rolls on the dust, whose
Befallen souls are bent downward,

Paper, all these times I have spoken
To you--
You have given me company in silence
Within your pleasure you have held up there
All variety collections of words of this pen,

And, you left me ever indebted
To you---
For a long while in the turmoil of time
In the ups and downs of this mind villa
You have extended your heart
To have my writings engraved
Into your chest--
To carry it to humans over the horizon,

The ever-unsatisfied pen of mine
Climbing the top of the heart, ran
From this sunset to that red glow of sunrise
With an expectation to check that the
Advancement deprived human's conditions lives
Are not being toppled altogether,

Paper, all these times I have spoken words
With you--
Today the opportunity has come, I have achieved the right
In this exalted invitational gathering
I will bring up
The issue of neglected, tortured and fallen to the ground humans
In this noble gathering of talented people of civilized world,

But suddenly, in the back of my mind, I look
Opening the door of the heart
I search and find nothing new in there
Worth saying--
All the tortures, all the oppressions
The peak of the sufferings

Of different kinds of different size and type
Upon the souls of the human kind,
All of these I have said from time beginning to the end,

But then, I pronounce in this gathering,
The running horse of civilization
Into your ears and eyes alike
The deceiving cover needs to be removed
Otherwise, in a civilization without humans
You will be drowning with a struggle going above and under water
And ah! You will be only one to remain.

August 17, 2003
Port Washington, NY 11050

A PIECE OF PAPER

Bengali: 'Tookrow Kagoj'

I am a piece of paper
Lying haphazardly
Upon the chest of the public thoroughfare,
I fly up and down with the slap of the wind
Within a little distance in the air
From the face of the earth.

Again, I wrap-around myself falling on the thoroughfare
My body gets rudely twisted,
The next moment the slap of the running vehicles
Throw me at a distance, sometimes lying on the dusts
And, sometimes again, waving in the air
Like the falling kite with the broken string from its reel
Upon the chest of the thoroughfare with a thud.

Sometimes, under the wheels of the passing vehicles
I am crushed and grinded,
Before I have a chance to breathe
The slap of another speedy vehicle
Lands on me again,
My head goes spinning wild
And revolving and revolving I fall down
Like a sunken drunk man.

Consuming these slaps from every shore all around
Many times
I pass across a little distance
On the thoroughfare.

Once in a while my fate is a little better
After a few strikes and slaps
I fall down and lay aside by the thoroughfare
Where the strikes from the speedy vehicles
Are not unfrustrated,
I keep lying down in a pellucid counting of time
And I see--
The blind speed of civilization in a careless eompetition
Leave me behind
In the soiled dust or by the filthy roadside
In an indomitable dire desire of senseless speedy advancement.

In dirty layers, I am a piece of paper
By that thoroughfare,
And the face impression of a human-piece
I behold in this path of the world
In the outskirt of this speedy advancing civilized world
Under its feet.

March 1, 2003
Port Washington, NY

A LITTLE BONDAGE

Bengali: 'Chotto Bandan'

It looks as if I am being captivated
By all these---
My whole self, my feelings,
This mind of mine that I have endured
To walk around
The side of slipped-off life-values of humans,

My nearest one, my neighbor, my neighbor of the world
Who are surrounding my heart
Whose memory is my travel companion
And it's just like the rhythm
Of the mind-warmth of every moment of the day,

It seems, they want to snatch me
Away to a distance
From my nerve connection with the human tide
After whose name this race, this nation
The holding plank of this solar system
The one and only solo strength of liberty, the robust song,

They are these ordinary general populace
The tune of inspiration of my songs
The charming fine arts of endurance of tune
Who still are saddened by the burden of heavy sorrows
The mere utterance of which spreads displeasure in the mind.

April 1999
Port Washington, New York